The Bedtime Book of Magical Creatures

An introduction to more than 100 creatures from legend and folklore

Written by: Stephen Krensky
Illustrated by: Katarzyna Doszla, Lucy Semple, Paula Zamudio, Sara Ugolotti

Contents

In the air

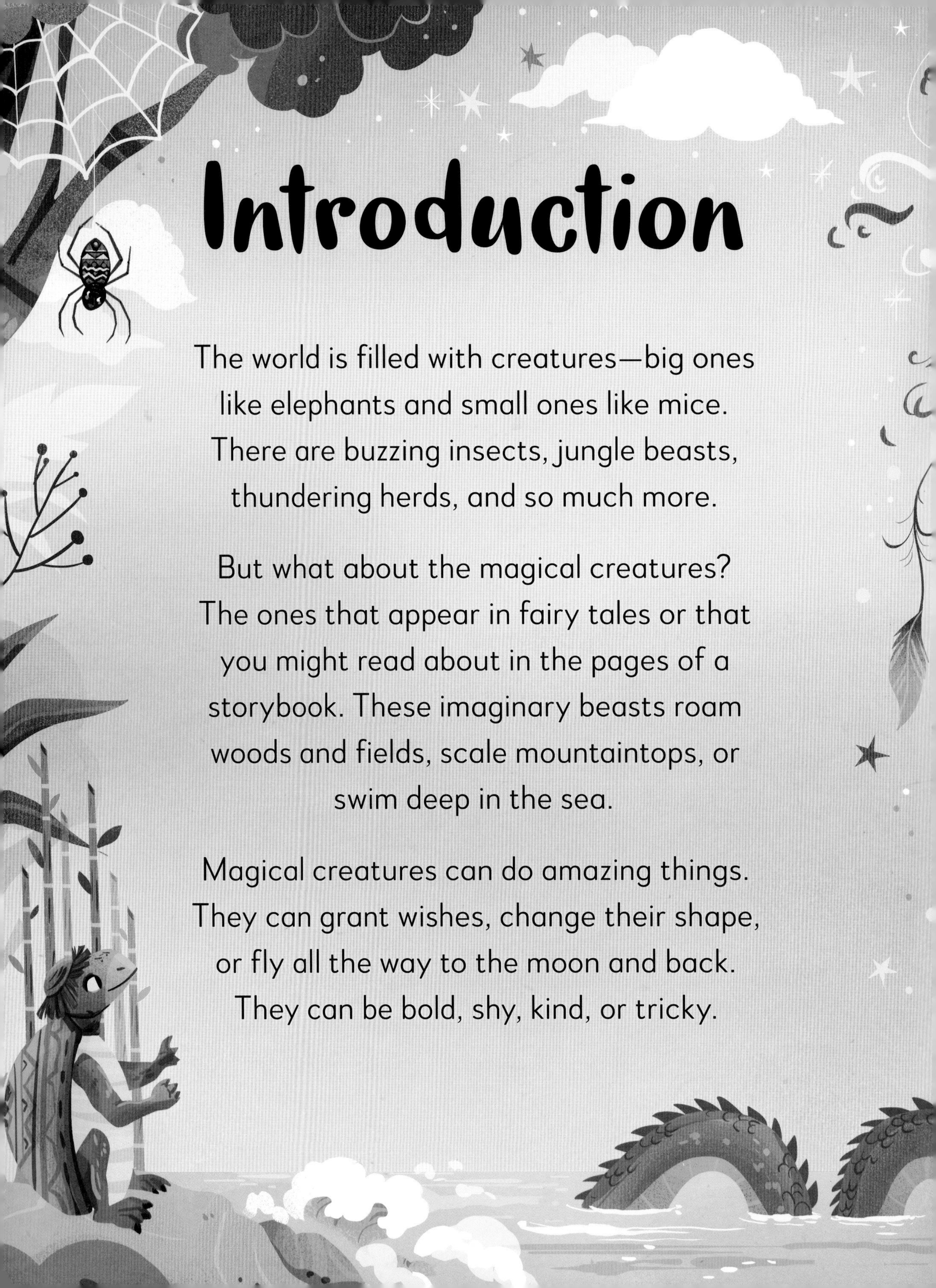

Introduction

The world is filled with creatures—big ones like elephants and small ones like mice. There are buzzing insects, jungle beasts, thundering herds, and so much more.

But what about the magical creatures? The ones that appear in fairy tales or that you might read about in the pages of a storybook. These imaginary beasts roam woods and fields, scale mountaintops, or swim deep in the sea.

Magical creatures can do amazing things. They can grant wishes, change their shape, or fly all the way to the moon and back. They can be bold, shy, kind, or tricky.

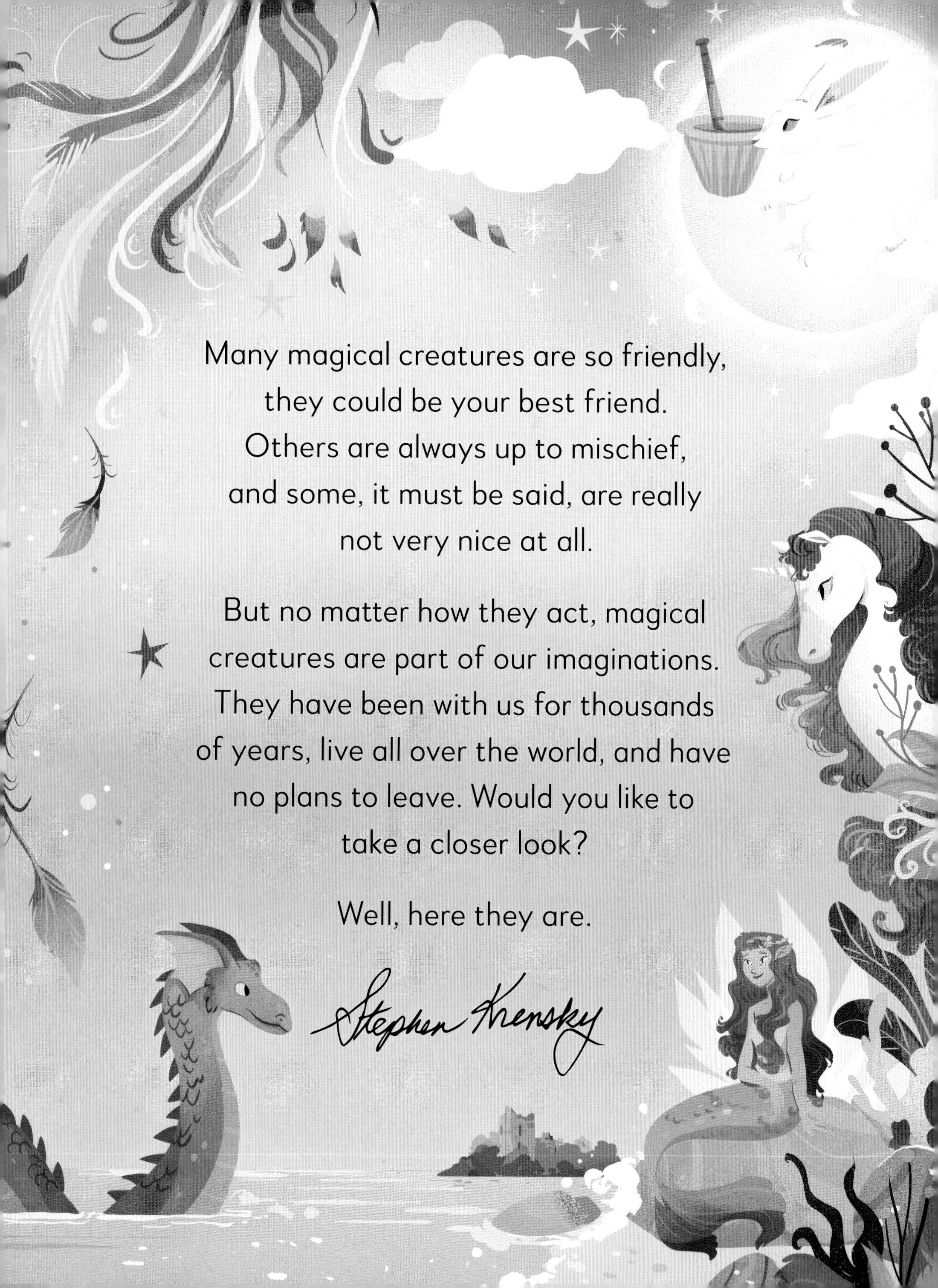

Many magical creatures are so friendly, they could be your best friend. Others are always up to mischief, and some, it must be said, are really not very nice at all.

But no matter how they act, magical creatures are part of our imaginations. They have been with us for thousands of years, live all over the world, and have no plans to leave. Would you like to take a closer look?

Well, here they are.

Stephen Krensky

On land

Magical creatures that live on land can cover a lot of ground. They may live on high mountains or settle in dry deserts. They might spend their time in the treetops or the short, green grasses of open fields.

Wherever these creatures live, they don't all move across the land in the same way. Many walk or run or gallop. Others prefer to slink or roll or jump.

Some of these mythical creatures have much in common. There are several different magical cats, for instance, and quite a few legendary lizards and snakes.

Other creatures appear to have been assembled from a mix of claws, tails, and furry legs that nobody seems to have planned very carefully. Sometimes these combinations make sense—but not always. Still, the result is a unique magical creature that is often unforgettable.

Fauns love to play happy tunes on wooden flutes.

Faun like to have **parties**, and anyone who comes across one is welcome to join in.

Faun

A faun is a man from the waist up and a **goat** from the waist down. Fauns spend most of their time playing music and dancing in the woods.

Satyr

Satyrs are like fauns in many ways, and are also half-goat and half-man. However, satyrs are **hairier** than fauns, and it must be said they are sneakier, too.

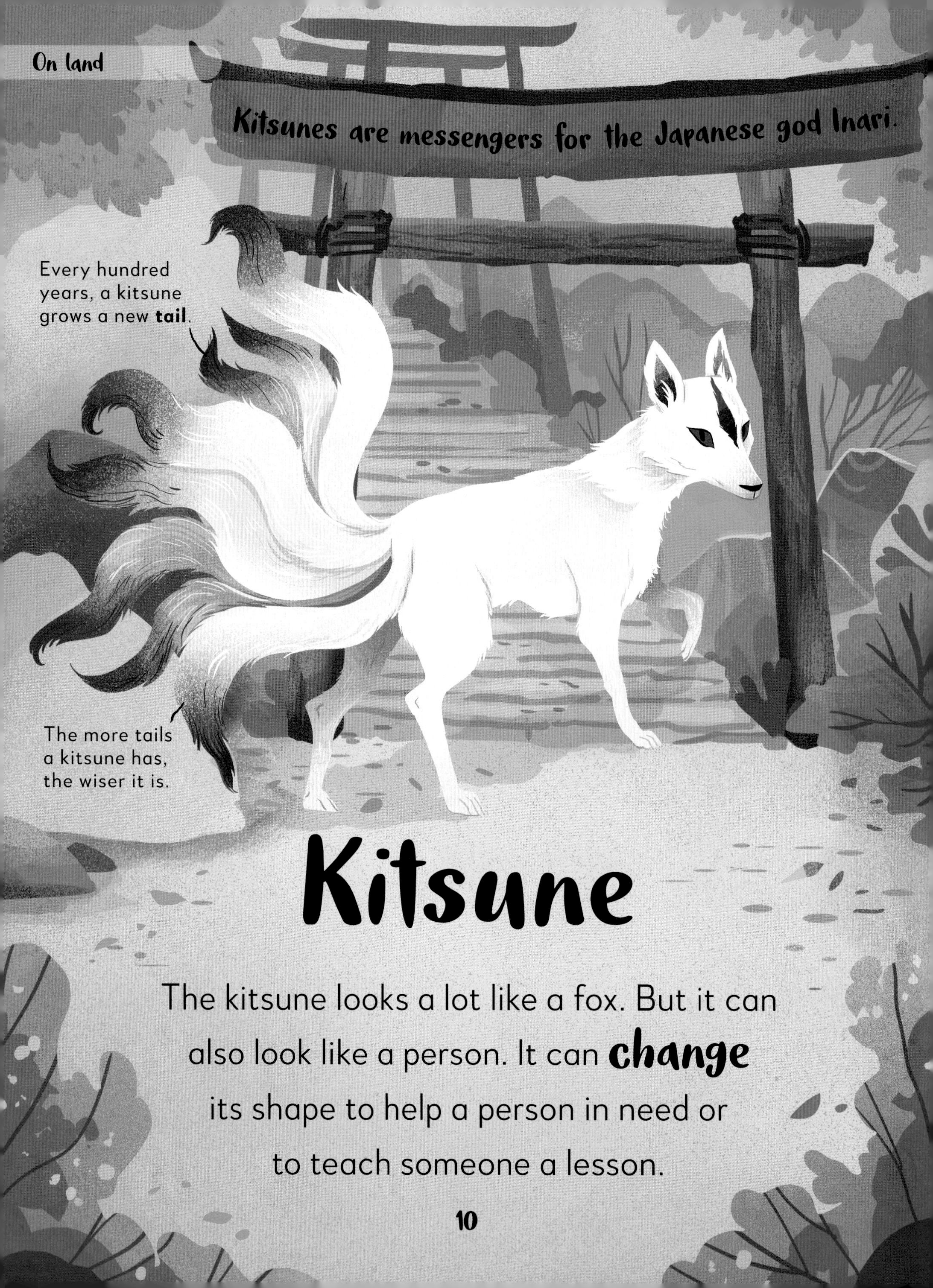

Kitsunes are messengers for the Japanese god Inari.

Every hundred years, a kitsune grows a new **tail**.

The more tails a kitsune has, the wiser it is.

Kitsune

The kitsune looks a lot like a fox. But it can also look like a person. It can **change** its shape to help a person in need or to teach someone a lesson.

Sibuxiang

The Chinese sibuxiang looks like the pieces of an animal **puzzle** all mixed together. It has the hooves of a cow, the antlers of a deer, the tail of a donkey, and a head like a horse.

"Sibuxiang" means "four ways of being unalike".

Deer's antlers

Donkey's tail

Horselike head

The sibuxiang is based on a **real** animal called the Père David's deer.

Cow's hooves

Minotaur

The Minotaur has the body of a man and the head of a bull. He was so dangerous that he was kept a **prisoner** in a stone maze called the Labyrinth.

Babe the Blue Ox

Babe the Blue Ox was the pet of Paul Bunyan, the legendary lumberjack of North America. Babe was **blue** from birth, and his color never changed even when he was nice and warm.

Gamusino

The gamusino is a small furry creature that is hard to find. Some people claim the gamusino can be hunted at **night**, but these same people have never caught one.

The gamusino may look like a **pet**, but it is not tame.

The gamusino is well known in Spain and Portugal.

Large eyes

Clawlike feet

Golem

A golem starts out as a small **clay** creature. What happens after that depends on who is making it. If it's a good person, the golem will be good. If it's a bad person, there could be trouble.

Goblin

Goblins are **greedy**. They like gold and jewels, and can never have too much of them. They will stop at nothing to get rich.

One goblin knew how to spin straw into gold—his name was **Rumpelstiltskin**.

Dwarf

A dwarf is short, stocky, and very strong. Dwarfs live underground, where they go **mining** for gold and jewels. They turn these riches into goblets and other treasures.

Elf

Elves are kindly creatures who make their home in the forest. They care deeply about **nature** and like to protect it.

Gnomes often like to wear **pointed** hats.

Gnome

Goblinlike gnomes once lived underground, searching for treasure. But some of them decided to come up for fresh air and take care of **gardens**.

The story of Ymir is based on an ancient Norse poem from the lands of **Scandinavia**.

Ymir

All giants are big, but Ymir is the **biggest**. The earth was made from his flesh, the sea from his sweat, the mountains from his bones, the trees from his hair, and the sky from his skull.

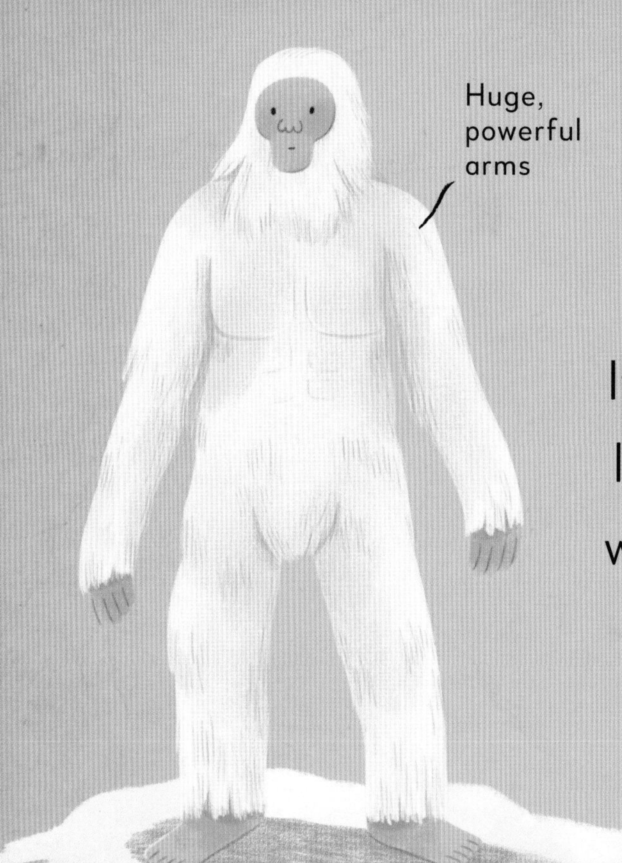

Yeti

If you were a cross between a large brown bear and an ape, where would you want to live? The yeti picks the highest **mountains** in Asia.

Another name for Bigfoot is Sasquatch.

Bigfoot

Bigfoot is not a creature with one big foot. He actually has two big feet. They are attached to two very large and **hairy** legs.

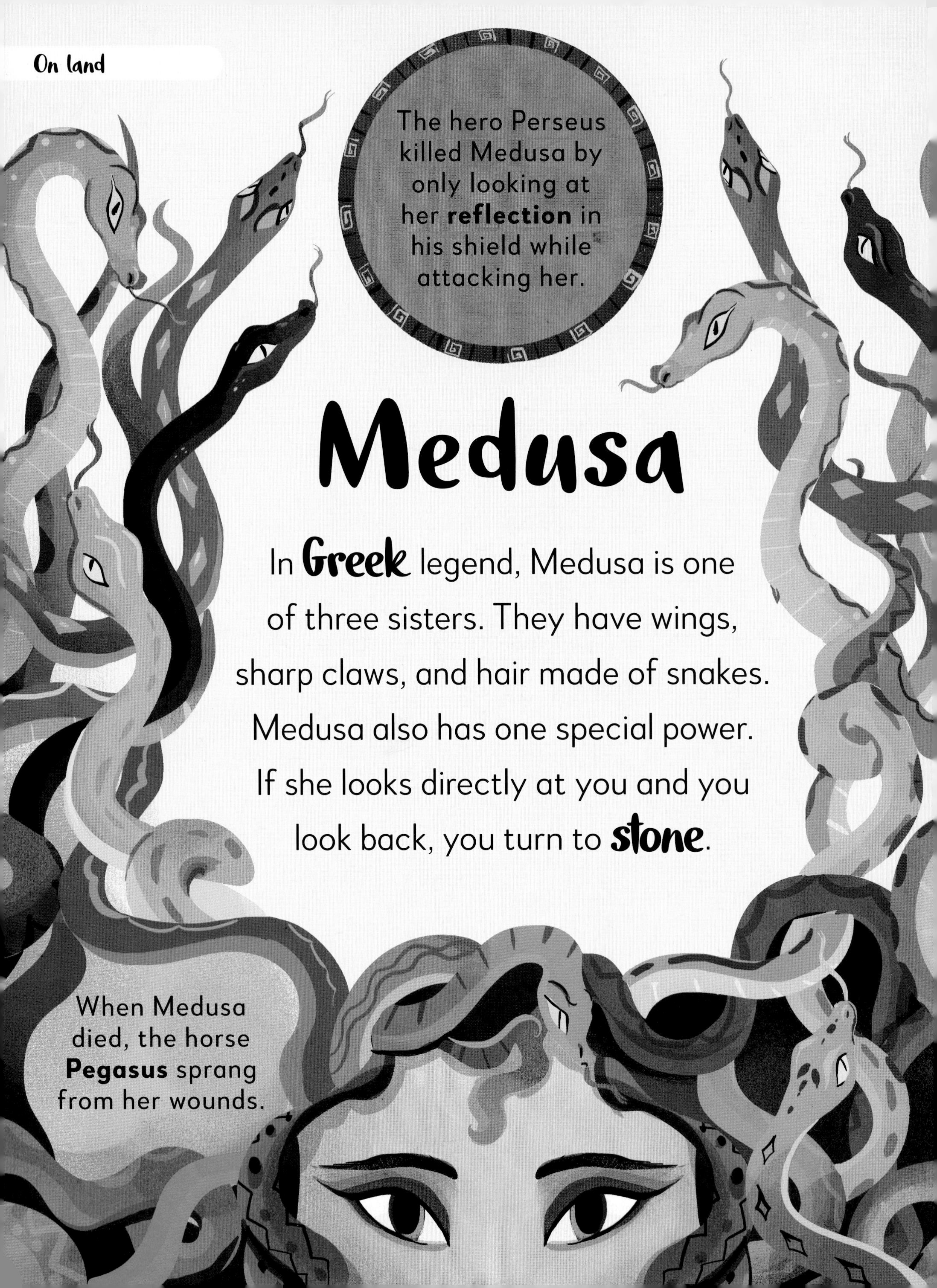

The hero Perseus killed Medusa by only looking at her **reflection** in his shield while attacking her.

Medusa

In **Greek** legend, Medusa is one of three sisters. They have wings, sharp claws, and hair made of snakes. Medusa also has one special power. If she looks directly at you and you look back, you turn to **stone**.

When Medusa died, the horse **Pegasus** sprang from her wounds.

Ammit was the ancient Egyptian goddess of the Underworld.

It was believed that **scales** were used to help pass judgment.

Ammit

Ammit was a **goddess** of ancient Egypt. She helped judge what happened to people's spirits after they died. If a person's heart was lighter than a feather, it was believed they became immortal.

Fenrir

Like many wolves in folklore, Fenrir **howls** at the moon.

Fenrir is a mighty wolf. He is the child of a clever and powerful Norse god called **Loki**. The other gods feared Fenrir and imprisoned him in magical chains.

Fenrir's chains are stronger than any metal.

One day, Fenrir will break free and cause a lot of trouble.

The qilin has been compared to the **giraffe**. They don't look very alike, but they do both have horns, a mane, and thick eyelashes.

Qilin

The qilin might look a little scary, but it is actually very **gentle**. According to Chinese legend, the qilin often appears at the birth or death of a wise person or great ruler.

Airavata

Elephants have one trunk, but Airavata of Hindu mythology has **several**. He is a symbol of strength and helps protect everyone from evil.

Indra, the king of the gods, rode Airavata into battle. They fought the great serpent **Vritra** with thunderbolts to free the waters of the earth.

Unlike other elephants, Airavata is **pure** white.

Airavata has several other names, including Elephant of the Gods and the Fighting Elephant.

Unicorn

This noble creature looks like a small horse, but there is one important difference. It has a **single horn** on its head.

Anansi

Anansi is no ordinary **spider**! He made the sun, moon, and all the sparkling stars in the sky. He also brought **stories** into the world.

Anansi collected the world's wisdom and put it in a **calabash** bowl. Some of it spilled out, so Anansi shared the wisdom with all people.

Anansi is a much-loved animal trickster from West African myth.

Alux

An alux is a sprite about knee-high. It is often invisible, and is only rarely seen. The alux doesn't like to be talked about. So, if one helps you, just thank it **silently**.

Chanekeh

Chanekeh are the size of children, although they look a bit like elderly people. They are known to play **tricks**, such as leading people into places where they might get lost.

Stories of the chanekeh were first told by the **Aztec** people of Mexico.

Chanekeh are often found near forests, rivers, or caves.

It was widely believed that a person might turn into a werewolf by the light of the **full moon**.

Werewolves first appeared in **Europe** thousands of years ago.

Werewolf

A werewolf is part wolf and part human. It's said that a person becomes a werewolf when **bitten** by one. So, it's best to run away from any werewolves you see.

Chimera

Chimera is a very odd beast. It has **three heads**—the head of a lion, the head of a goat, and the head of a snake, which sticks out at the back of its body. It can even breathe fire.

Chimera fought with many warriors of **ancient Greek** legend.

Cats

Cats are known for their independence and have a sense of **mystery** about them. They have also been much appreciated because they like to eat mice.

It is said that the **cat sith** of Scottish myth can steal dead people's souls after they die.

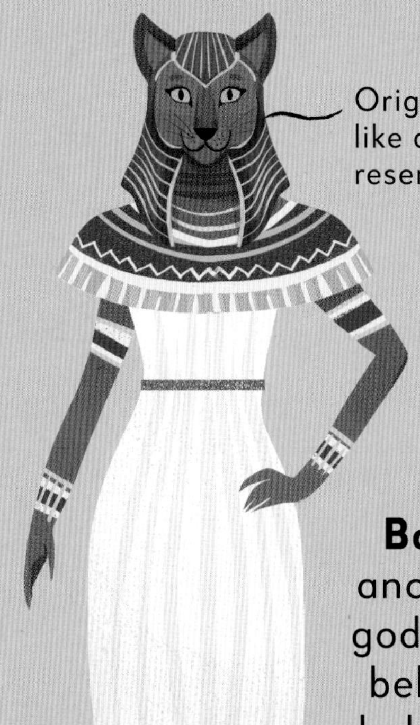

Bastet was an ancient Egyptian goddess. She was believed to be a helpful protector from evil spirits and diseases.

Puss in Boots is not like any other cat. He walks on his two back legs and wears fancy clothes, including tall leather boots. He is also clever, and helps his owner marry a princess.
The **cactus cat** makes its home in the desert. It looks like a bobcat—except it's covered in thorns, not hair. It also has an armored tail.
Puss in Boots
Cactus cat
The **Cheshire Cat** is a big cat, often found sitting on the branch of a tree. He is known for his wide, mischievous grin.
The Cheshire Cat who meets Alice in Wonderland can make himself **disappear**—so all that's left is his smile.
Cheshire Cat

Sun Wukong was a **warrior** at first, but later he became a monkey of **peace**.

Sun Wukong

When your nickname is the **Monkey King**, you have to be tough—really tough. And Sun Wukong is just that. He can carry a mountain on his back. He can out-race a meteor. He can even freeze his enemies with magic.

Sphinx

The ancient Egyptian sphinx has a human's head and a lion's body. The people of ancient Egypt thought the sphinx would guard them and keep them safe. So, they built a lot of **statues** to honor it.

Carbuncle

The carbuncle loves **jewels**. It likes them so much, it has a red one sticking out of its forehead. Carbuncles live near mines, where they can collect more jewels when they get the chance.

Carbuncles may look like cats or foxes. They are hard to **catch**, so it's difficult to know for sure.

Carbuncles live in South America—especially **Chile**.

Puca

Pucas have been seen roaming around the **British Isles**.

The puca can **change shape**. It may look like a cat, a dog, or some farm animals. It can even pretend to be a person, but one with pointed ears and a tail. Why go to all this trouble? Changing shape helps the puca play tricks on people.

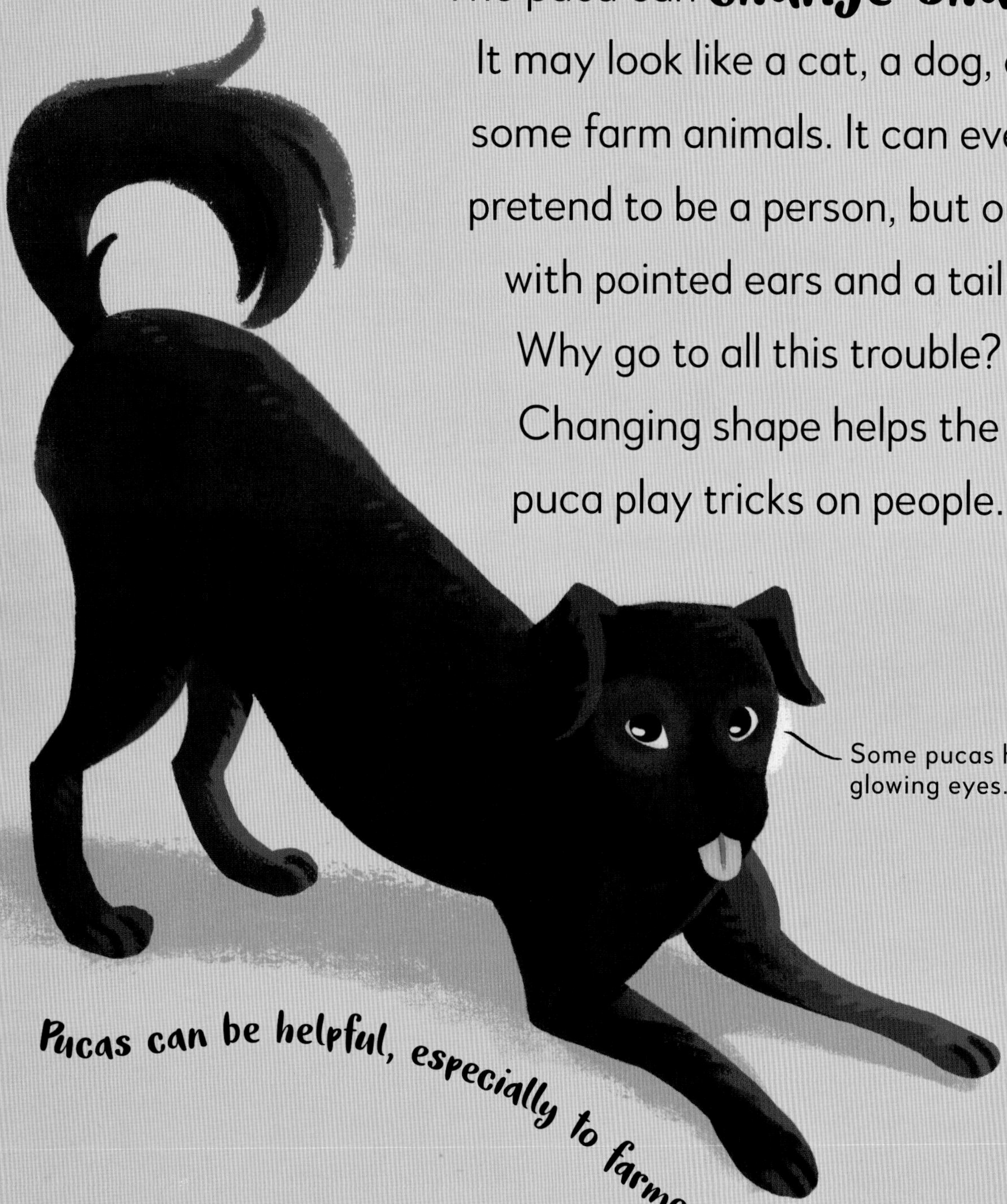

Some pucas have glowing eyes.

Pucas can be helpful, especially to farmers.

Gogmagog was the last giant to live in the British Isles.

Gogmagog appears in Welsh and English **folklore**.

Gogmagog was so strong that he could pull an **oak tree** out of the earth with just one hand.

Gogmagog

Like all **giants**, Gogmagog was really big. He lived with other giants that did whatever they pleased. Finally, a brave soldier wrestled with Gogmagog and threw him off the edge of a cliff.

Jackalope

The jackalope looks like a **jackrabbit** with antelope horns on the front of its head. Luckily, its neck is strong enough to hold the extra weight. Jackalopes are shy, and nobody has ever captured one.

The name jackalope is a mixture of jackrabbit and antelope.

Sightings of the jackalope have been limited to the western plains of **North America**.

Tanuki

The tanuki looks like a raccoon and a dog put together. This little creature is full of **mischief**. It can change its shape at will, and likes to play tricks on people.

Brownie

A brownie gets its name because it wears brown clothes. Brownies sneak into people's homes at night. There, they **clean up** and help out in different ways.

Imp

An imp is a bony little **demon**. It is not evil, but it does like to play tricks on people. And when it does this, it wears a sneaky smile on its face.

Leprechaun

A leprechaun is a small bearded man who likes to make and repair shoes. If you catch a leprechaun, he will grant you three **wishes** to let him go.

His greatest love is **gold**, which he often stores at the end of a rainbow.

Pixie

Pixies wear pointed hats that match their pointed ears. They spend most of their time outdoors, dancing and playing. If they get bored, they cast **charms** on people.

Pixies love to **wrestle** with one another.

Benandonner, also known as the Red Man, was angry a lot of the time, which made his face red.

Finn had a magic thumb that shared great wisdom with him.

Finn McCool and Benandonner

There were once two giants who didn't like each other. One, Finn McCool, lived in **Ireland**. The other, Benandonner, lived in **Scotland**. Finally, they decided to fight, and their battles changed the shape of their coastlines.

Big Bad Wolf

The Big Bad Wolf is not a magical wolf, but he is full of hot air. If he takes a really big breath, he can **blow** a house down. But not every house. A brick house is strong enough to stand against his blasts.

The Big Bad Wolf that bothers the **three little pigs** is not the same one that tried to eat Little Red Riding Hood, but they were both big and bad.

The white stag appears in **stories** throughout Europe and parts of Asia.

Powerful legs

With its shimmering coat, the white stag is a symbol of **purity**.

White stag

A white stag is **rare** for two reasons. One is because of its color. The other is because it is magical and cannot be caught. Some people believe the white stag is a messenger from a faraway world.

Snow Lion

The Snow Lion is the symbol of **Tibet**, a region high in the Himalayan mountains. It is one of four mythical creatures of Buddhism that represent strength, confidence, and cheerfulness.

It is too cold in Tibet for ordinary lions to live there.

A single **roar** from the Snow Lion may cause seven dragons to fall from the sky.

Atlas never got to go away on vacation because he had to hold up the sky all the time.

Atlas

Atlas was an ancient Greek giant. All giants are big, but Atlas was bigger than most. He actually held the **whole sky** on his shoulders. It was very heavy, but he was being punished for rebelling against Zeus, the king of the gods. So, he was not allowed to complain.

Atlas was the god of **strength**, but he would have been happier not to have to prove it.

Crone

A crone is an aged woman who can perform **magic**. She wears dark-colored clothes and a tall pointed hat. Crones are not always disagreeable, but most of them are.

Crones tend to live in the **forests** of Europe.

Crones usually have only a **black cat** for company.

Kalku

A kalku is a powerful **sorceress** who lives in parts of South America. She doesn't have to be evil, but she often isn't nice and doesn't make friends easily.

Baba Yaga

Baby Yaga is a Russian **witch** who lives deep in the woods. If you meet her, be prepared. You may be asked to do something for her. Make sure you can do it! If you fail, you may have to stay for dinner—her dinner.

Mangkukulam

Some witches are good and some are bad. The mangkukulam are among the bad ones. They use **magic** to make themselves feared. And they will curse anyone who gets in their way.

The first trolls appear in stories from northern Europe.

The Three Billy Goats Gruff is a Norwegian story about a **grumpy** troll who argues with three goats.

Troll

Trolls come in big and small sizes. Sometimes they live in caves or under bridges. They like **dark** or shady places because many of them turn to stone in the sunlight. This makes them nervous.

Dokkaebi

A dokkaebi looks like a mean **goblin**. It has sharp horns, bulging eyes, and lots of hair. It is usually harmless unless you try to trick it. If you do that, and the dokkaebi finds out, you'll be sorry.

Stories about the dokkaebi were told in **Korea** for hundreds of years before they were written down.

Cyclops

A cyclops was a kind of giant. But as big as cyclopes were, each of them had only **one eye**. This eye was big, though, and was hard to miss. Cyclopes were scary enough already—having only one eye just made them look worse.

In an ancient Greek story, one cyclops was blinded by the hero **Odysseus**.

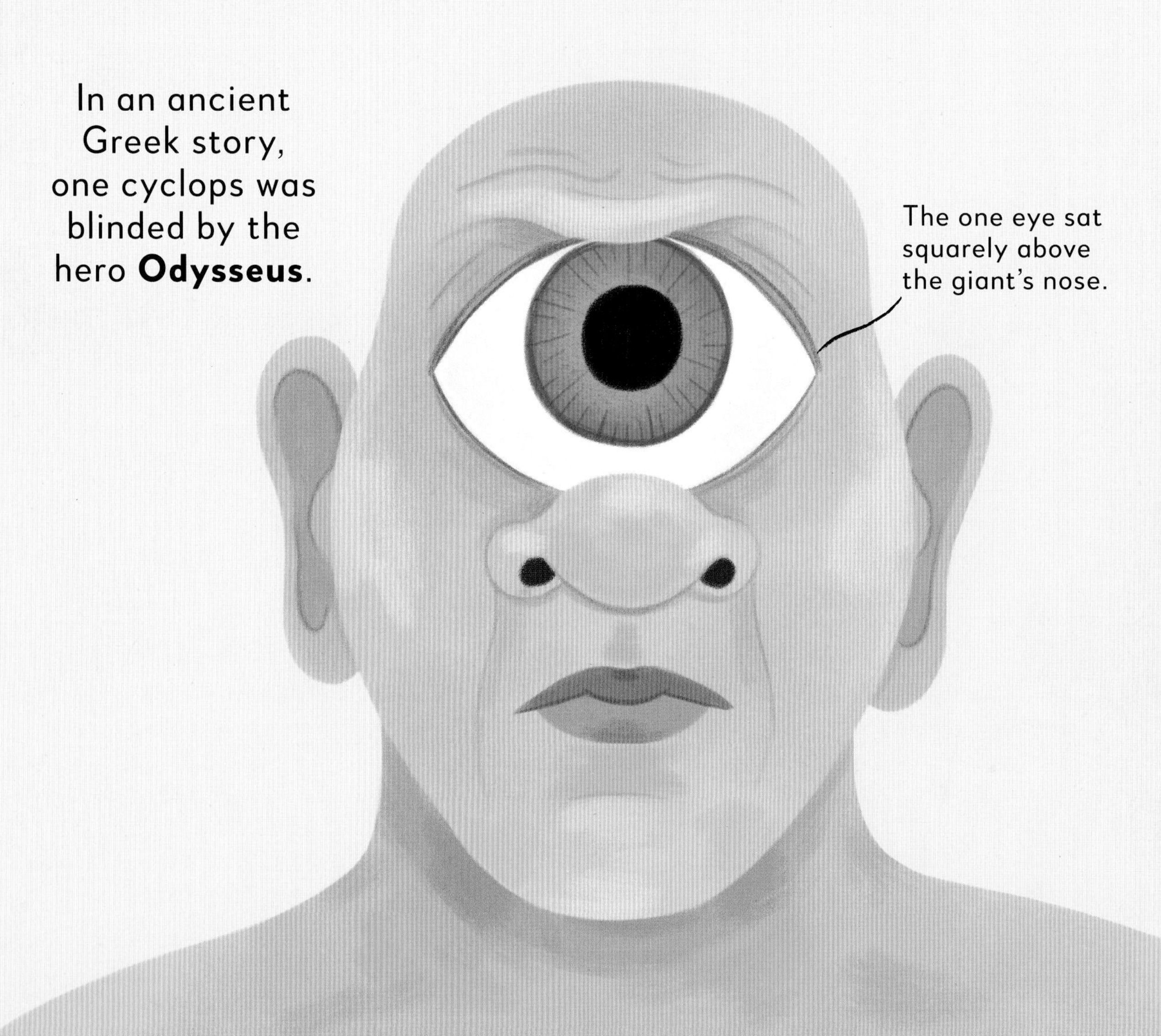

Hoop snakes are reported to have rolled around in **North America** and **Australia**.

The hoop snake rolls around when looking for something to eat.

Hoop snake

The hoop snake got its name because it can do one thing normal snakes can't do. It can **grab** its tail in its mouth and roll around like a **hoop**. This is much faster than slithering around.

Sometimes, the hoop snake will sting its prey with the stinger in its tail.

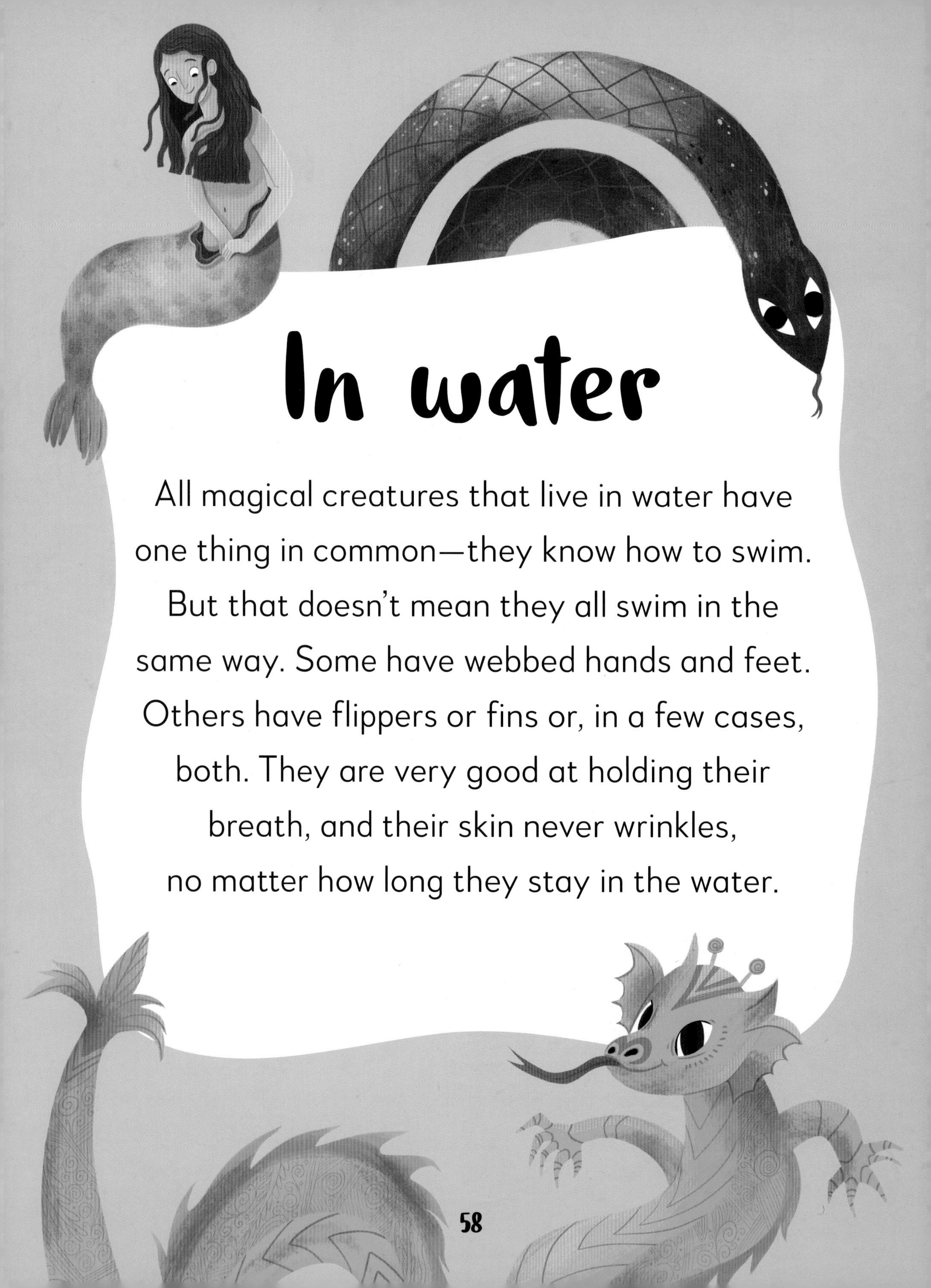

In water

All magical creatures that live in water have one thing in common—they know how to swim. But that doesn't mean they all swim in the same way. Some have webbed hands and feet. Others have flippers or fins or, in a few cases, both. They are very good at holding their breath, and their skin never wrinkles, no matter how long they stay in the water.

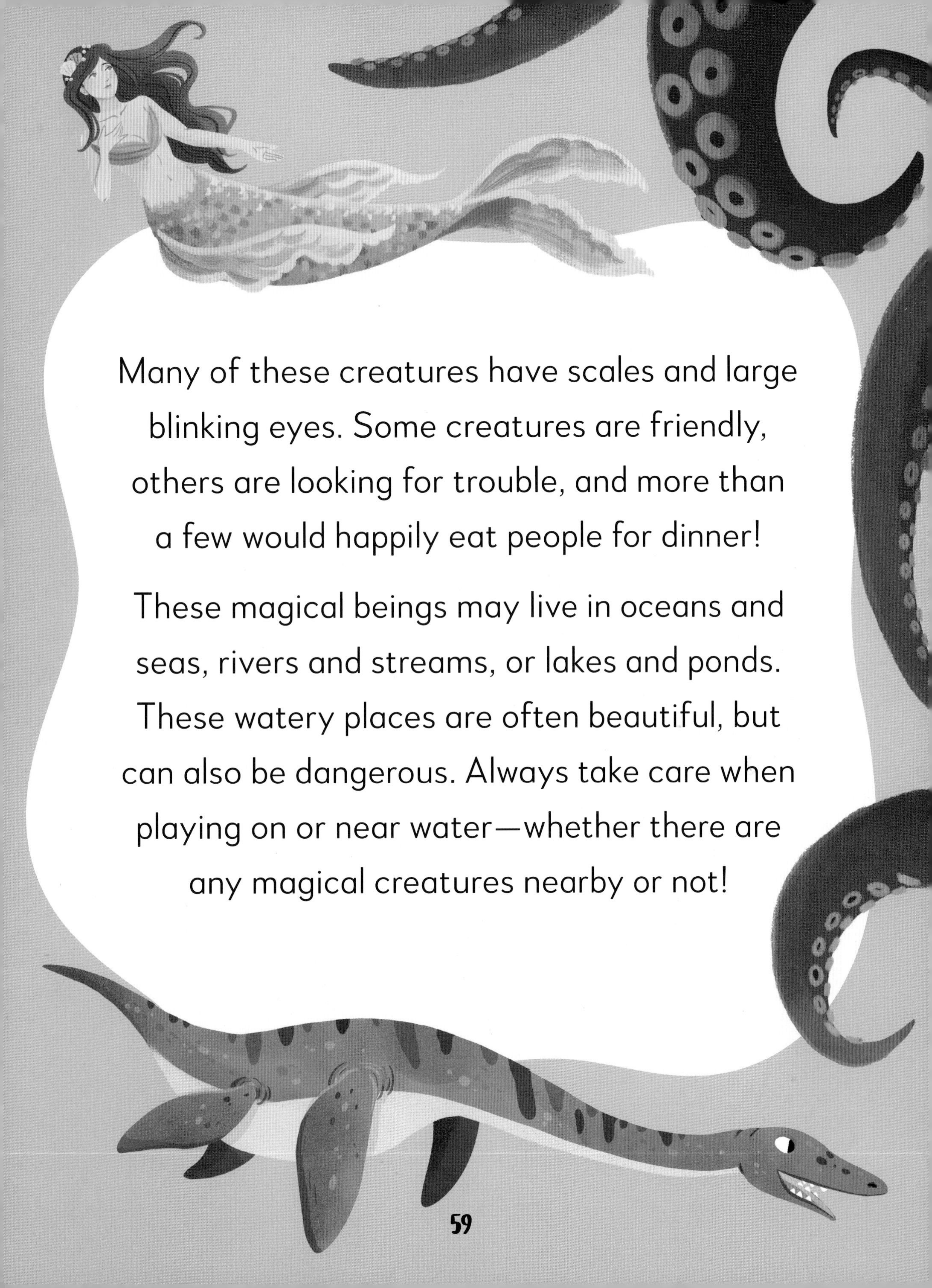

Many of these creatures have scales and large blinking eyes. Some creatures are friendly, others are looking for trouble, and more than a few would happily eat people for dinner!

These magical beings may live in oceans and seas, rivers and streams, or lakes and ponds. These watery places are often beautiful, but can also be dangerous. Always take care when playing on or near water—whether there are any magical creatures nearby or not!

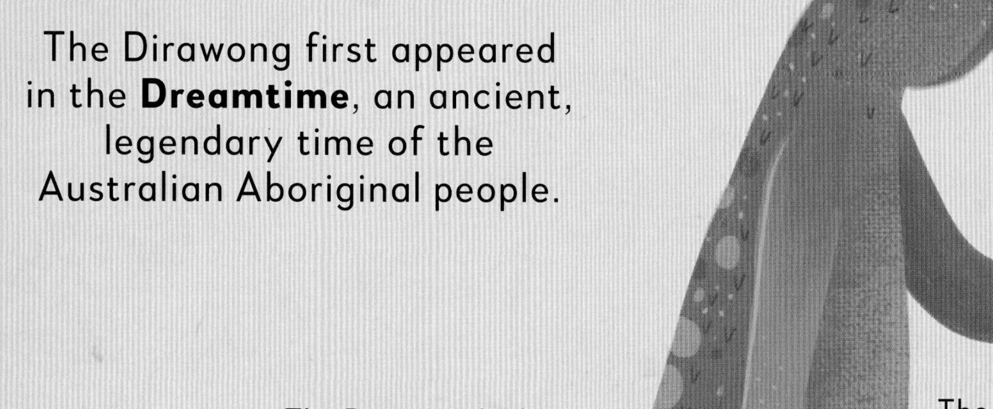

The Dirawong first appeared in the **Dreamtime**, an ancient, legendary time of the Australian Aboriginal people.

The Dirawong looks like a real-life **goanna lizard**, only bigger.

The Dirawong's sharp **claws** helped it fight the Rainbow Serpent.

Dirawong

In Australian Aboriginal folklore, the Dirawong is a large **lizard** with a long neck and sharp claws. Dirawong was a great teacher and protector that battled the Rainbow Serpent.

Rainbow Serpent

The huge snake known as the Rainbow Serpent was first seen pushing its way up through the earth. It then fought the Dirawong. The battle was so big and so fierce, it reshaped the coast of **Australia**.

Ryujin

Ryujin is the Japanese **dragon** that rules the seas. He has two homes. One is a palace in the sea. The other is in the lake of a sleeping volcano.

Glaucus

Glaucus started out in life as a Greek fisherman. Then he found a **magical herb** that brought dead fish back to life. He tried eating it, and the herb changed him into an immortal merman.

Glaucus has long hair and a beard.

Glaucus often helps fishermen in need. He also **rescues** sailors lost at sea.

Like all merfolk, Glaucus can only live in oceans and seas.

Water bull

The water bull of Scotland is very big, and has red flaring **nostrils**. Although it lives in the sea, it will come out onto the land in the moonlight.

In Scottish Gaelic, the water bull is called "tarbh uisge".

Two big horns

Bright red nostrils

Sometimes the water bull takes on other **shapes**, but being a bull is the shape it likes best.

Kelpie

The kelpie is a very different creature from the water bull. It likes **fresh water** for one thing, and swims in the lochs—or lakes—of Scotland.

Mermaids love to sing songs while stretched out on rocks.

Mermaid

Mermaids are female creatures who spend their lives in the sea. A mermaid is a **woman** on the top half of her body and a **fish** on the bottom half.

Some mermaids sing hoping to lure sailors to **crash** their ships on the rocks. Others hope to make friends with fisherfolk or even fall in **love**.

Many **stories** have been told about mermaids all over the world.

Makara is a legendary creature of Hindu mythology.

Makara

The ocean is filled with dangers. Hindu people worship Makara, hoping this **sea dragon** will protect them. They would sometimes decorate boats with symbols of Makara.

Triton lived in a golden palace, deep under the ocean's surface.

Triton blew on a large **conch shell** to announce Poseidon's arrival.

Triton

Triton was an ancient Greek god of the oceans. His favorite weapon was a **trident**. This is a spear with three pointed ends. Triton acted as a messenger for his father, Poseidon.

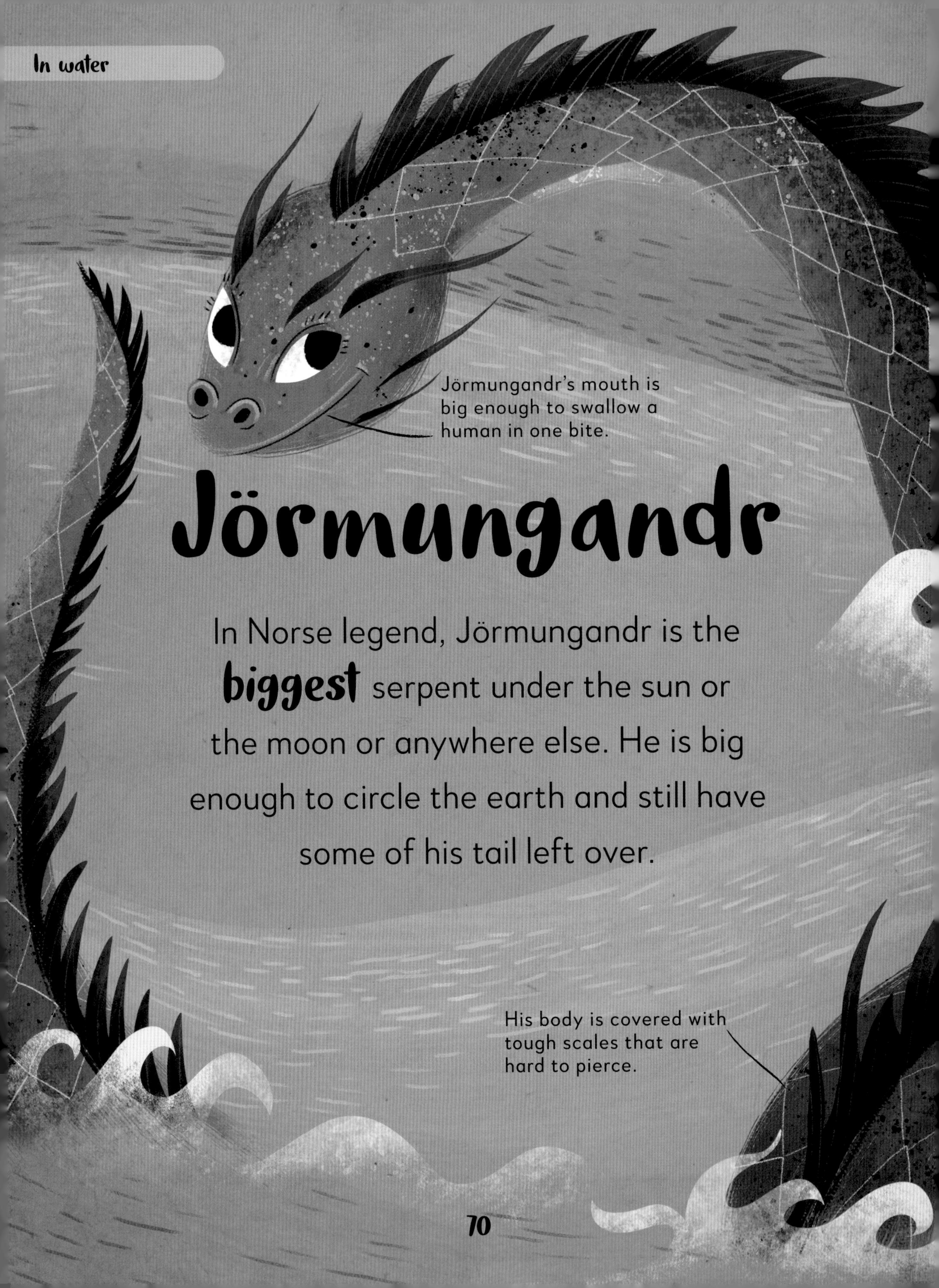

Jörmungandr

In Norse legend, Jörmungandr is the **biggest** serpent under the sun or the moon or anywhere else. He is big enough to circle the earth and still have some of his tail left over.

For a long time, Jörmungandr lived at the bottom of the **ocean**.

It was said that one day Jörmungandr would meet his **enemy**, Thor, the god of thunder, but that this day would not come for thousands of years.

Jörmungandr was first mentioned in stories about 2,000 years ago.

Hydra

Hydra is a **serpent** with nine heads. It also has poisonous breath and blood. If someone cuts off one of Hydra's heads, two more will grow in its place.

The Greek hero **Hercules** defeated Hydra. He told his servant to burn the neck of each head he cut off so that no more heads could grow.

Kappa

This little demon makes its home in the **rivers** and **ponds** of Japan. While always polite, the kappa can be **mischievous**, and has been known to play tricks on people.

The kappa has a bowl-like **dent** on its head that it needs to keep filled with water.

The kappa's favorite food is the cucumber.

The selkie lives on the northeastern isles of **Scotland.**

A selkie's worst nightmare is to **lose** its skin. If that happens, it is stuck on land and can't return to the sea.

Selkies can change their **shape** if they remove their skin.

The name "selkie" comes from the Scots word for "seal".

Selkie

This creature looks like a **seal** until it takes off its seal skin. Then it looks like a man or a woman. Selkies can be friendly, but if people try to catch them, they will fight back.

Pincoya

The pincoya is a beautiful **water spirit**. She lives at the bottom of the sea, off the coast of Chile, but she often comes up to visit the surface.

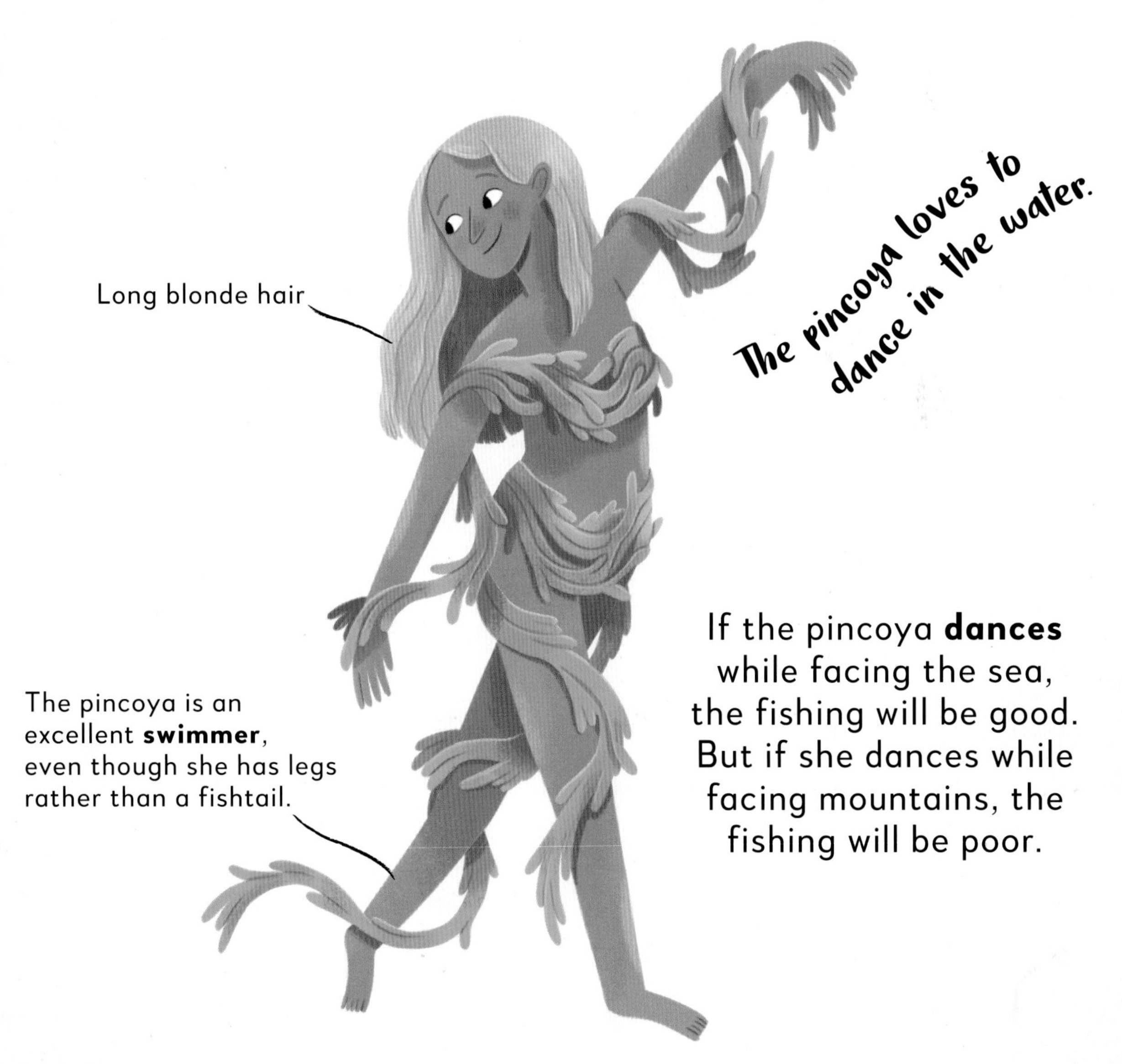

If the pincoya **dances** while facing the sea, the fishing will be good. But if she dances while facing mountains, the fishing will be poor.

Yakumama

The Yakumama is a really big **serpent**. How big? Big enough to swallow a person in just one bite! It also has blue scales and giant eyes that glow day or night.

The Yakumama was worshipped as a water spirit by the **Inca people** of South America

The sound of a conch shell is believed to disturb the Yakumama.

The ancient Greek sea god **Poseidon** never needed to be rescued, but hippocampi often pulled his chariot through the water.

The hippocampus is said to live in the Mediterranean Sea.

Hippocampus

The top half of a hippocampus looks like a **horse** and the bottom half is like a **fish**. This creature is a sailor's friend, because it often saves sailors from drowning or rescues them from sea monsters.

Merfolk

These creatures of the **sea** look human on the top half of their bodies, but have a **fishtail** on their bottom half. They live underwater, and just occasionally come on land.

Gulnare and the king have a **son** who can live on land or under the water.

These **mermen** have blue skin and live off the Scottish coast. Their cold hearts match the cold water, and they spend their time trying to **sink** passing ships.

Blue Men of the Minch

Gulnare of the Sea

Gulnare is a mysterious woman who captures the heart of a **Persian king**. After their marriage, the king learns that Gulnare comes from under the sea.

The Little Mermaid is the main character in a story of the same name by Hans Christian Andersen. She saves a human prince from drowning and then falls **in love** with him.

The Little Mermaid

These Chinese mermaids **weave** a brilliant white cloth that stays dry even underwater. When the jiaoren cry, their tears turn into **pearls**, which they can give away as gifts.

Jiaoren

The Japanese ningyo is part **human** and part **fish**, though the fish part is greater. They have bony clawlike fingers. The ningyo will put **curses** on anyone who tries to capture them.

Ningyo

Taniwha

Taniwha live in **pools** or **caves** near rivers and oceans. They are like giant lizards or dragons, with wings and scales. They can also change their shape to look like whales or sharks.

The Māori thought the taniwha could guide people through the waters between the North and South Islands of **New Zealand**.

Some people felt the taniwha would **protect** them. Others thought they were monsters that could attack on sight.

The ancient Greek hero, **Odysseus**, plugged his sailors' ears with wax so that they could not hear the song of the sirens.

Sirens have a woman's body and the wings and feet of a bird.

Sirens

These female creatures live near rocks and rushing waters. From there, they try to attract passing sailors. If the sailors listen to a **siren's song**, they often sail too close to the rocks and drown.

"Undine" comes from the Latin word for "wave."

An undine is a type of **nymph**. This is a female spirit linked with things in nature, such as trees and water.

Undine

Undines prefer freshwater pools and lakes to the ocean. They look female from the waist up. And if an undine should fall in love with a human, her **fishtail** will turn into legs.

Loch Ness Monster

The Loch Ness Monster, or **Nessie**, lives in Loch Ness, a lake in Scotland. Nessie is supposed to be very big. But she is also very shy.

Nessie has one or more **humps** that stick out of the water.

The Nahuelito is believed to have been spotted in **Nahuel Huapi Lake**.

This creature is said to look like a plesiosaur.

Nahuelito uses its **flippers** to swim.

Nahuelito

Stories have been told about this lake monster from **Argentina** for over a hundred years. The creature is thought to spend most of its time underwater, though it has never been seen.

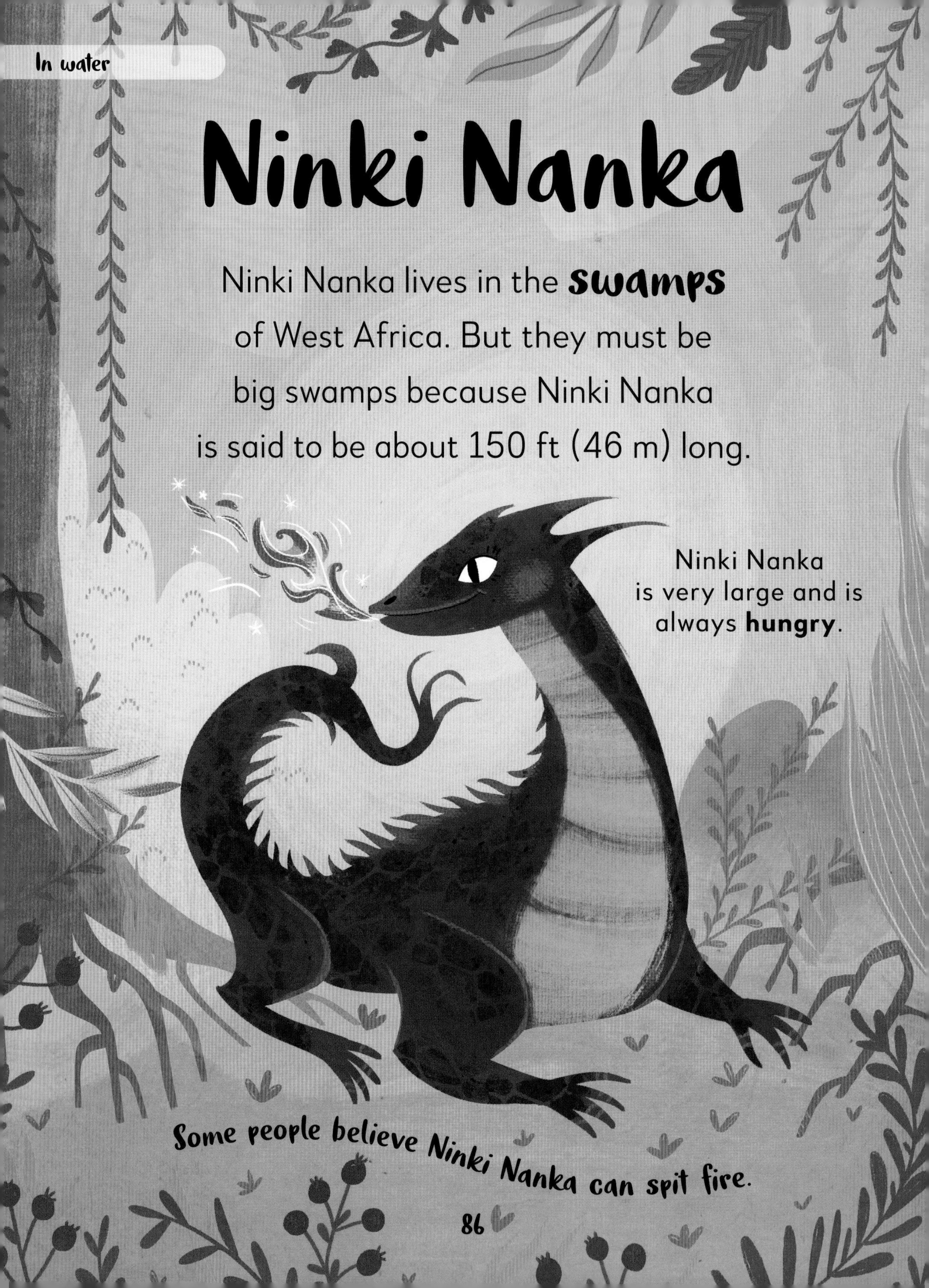

Ninki Nanka

Ninki Nanka lives in the **swamps** of West Africa. But they must be big swamps because Ninki Nanka is said to be about 150 ft (46 m) long.

Ninki Nanka is very large and is always **hungry**.

Some people believe Ninki Nanka can spit fire.

The Bake-Kujira spends most of its time near the water's surface even though it doesn't need to breathe.

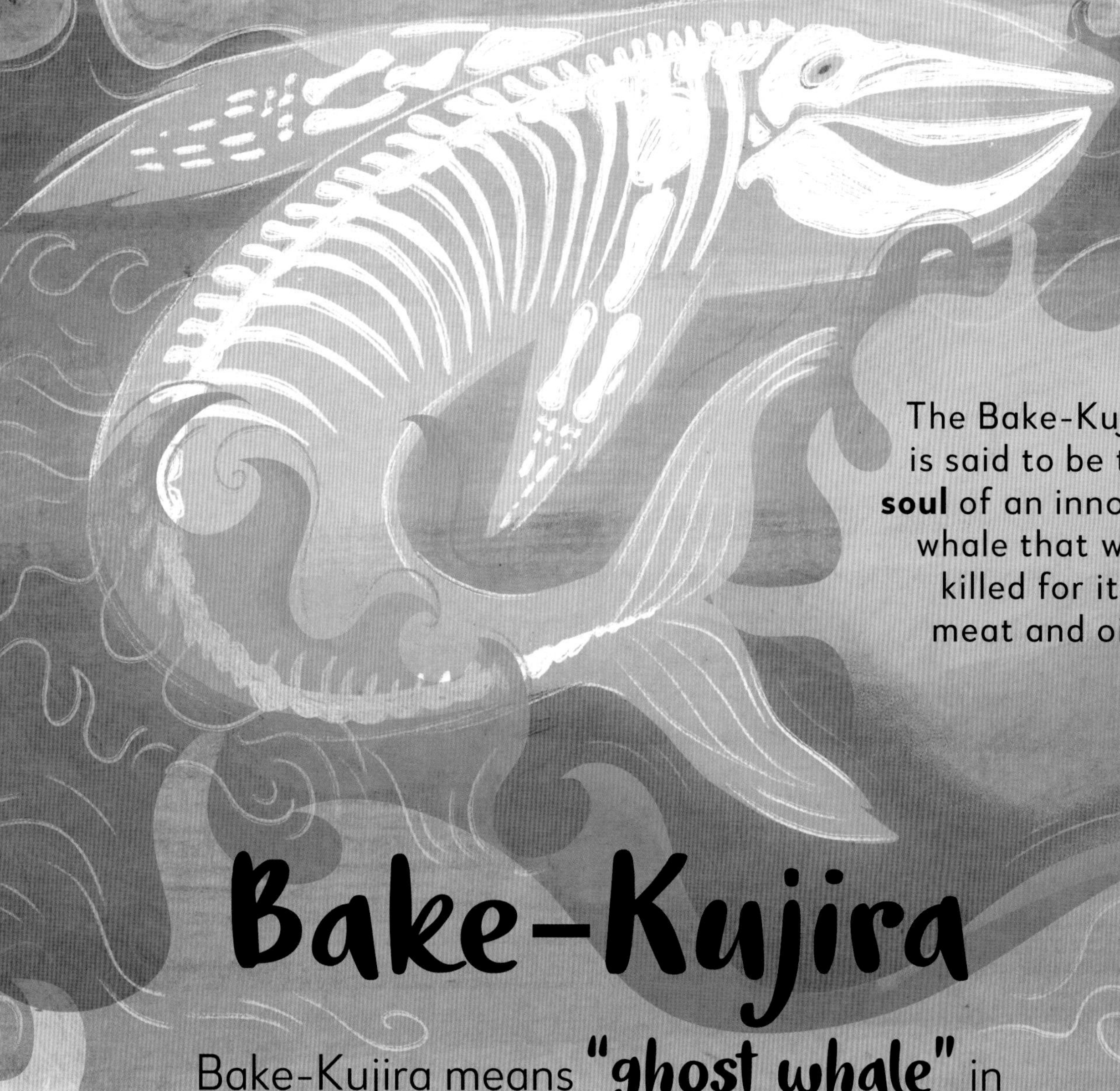

The Bake-Kujira is said to be the **soul** of an innocent whale that was killed for its meat and oil.

Bake-Kujira

Bake-Kujira means **"ghost whale"** in Japanese. However, it looks more like a whale skeleton than anything else. Birds and fish follow it wherever it goes.

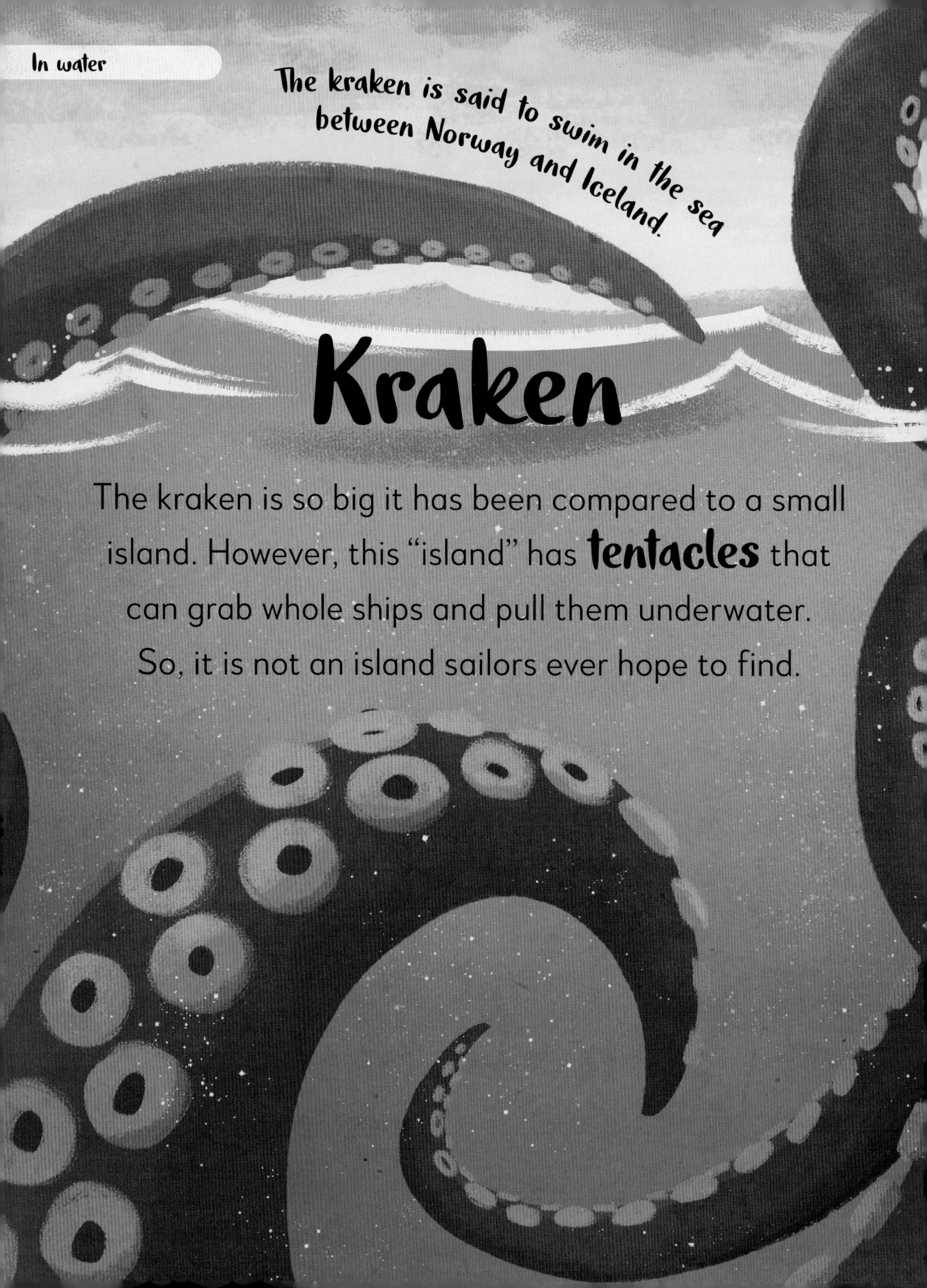

The kraken is said to swim in the sea between Norway and Iceland.

Kraken

The kraken is so big it has been compared to a small island. However, this "island" has **tentacles** that can grab whole ships and pull them underwater. So, it is not an island sailors ever hope to find.

The kraken only comes to the surface if it is **disturbed**. At that point it is too late for sailors to calm it down.

In the air

When we think of creatures flying through the air, we naturally think of birds. And while some flying magical creatures look like birds, there are many that don't.

Perhaps what makes the difference is their wings. Some creatures have feathery wings, like a bird's. Others have wings made of a thin skin stretched over bony joints.

However these creatures fly, they don't all do it the same way. Some can barely get off the ground—which may be all they need to do. Others do better, diving in loops and circles or whizzing around at blinding speeds. Are these displays always necessary? Or do these creatures enjoy showing off?

For others, flying is simply the best way to get from here to there. And, for the rest of us, it's not a bad idea to keep an eye on the sky. You never know when you might need to duck.

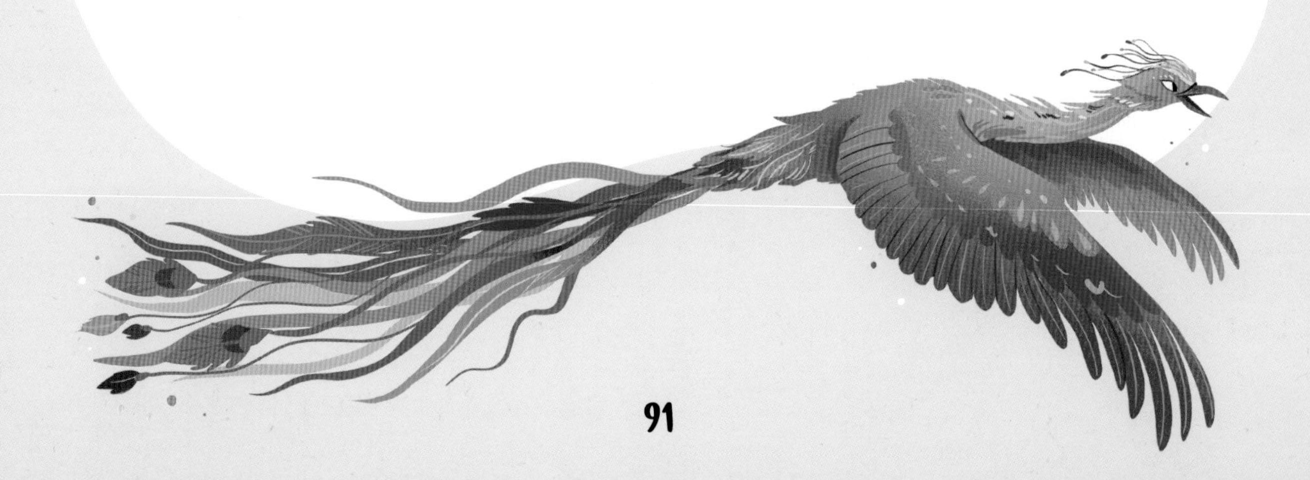

Phoenix

With its bright **fiery** feathers, huge wings, and long sharp beak, a giant bird called the phoenix rises from the ashes and is reborn again and again.

Bright orange feathers

Its eyes are usually blue, and shine like **sapphire** gems.

The phoenix symbolizes hope and rebirth.

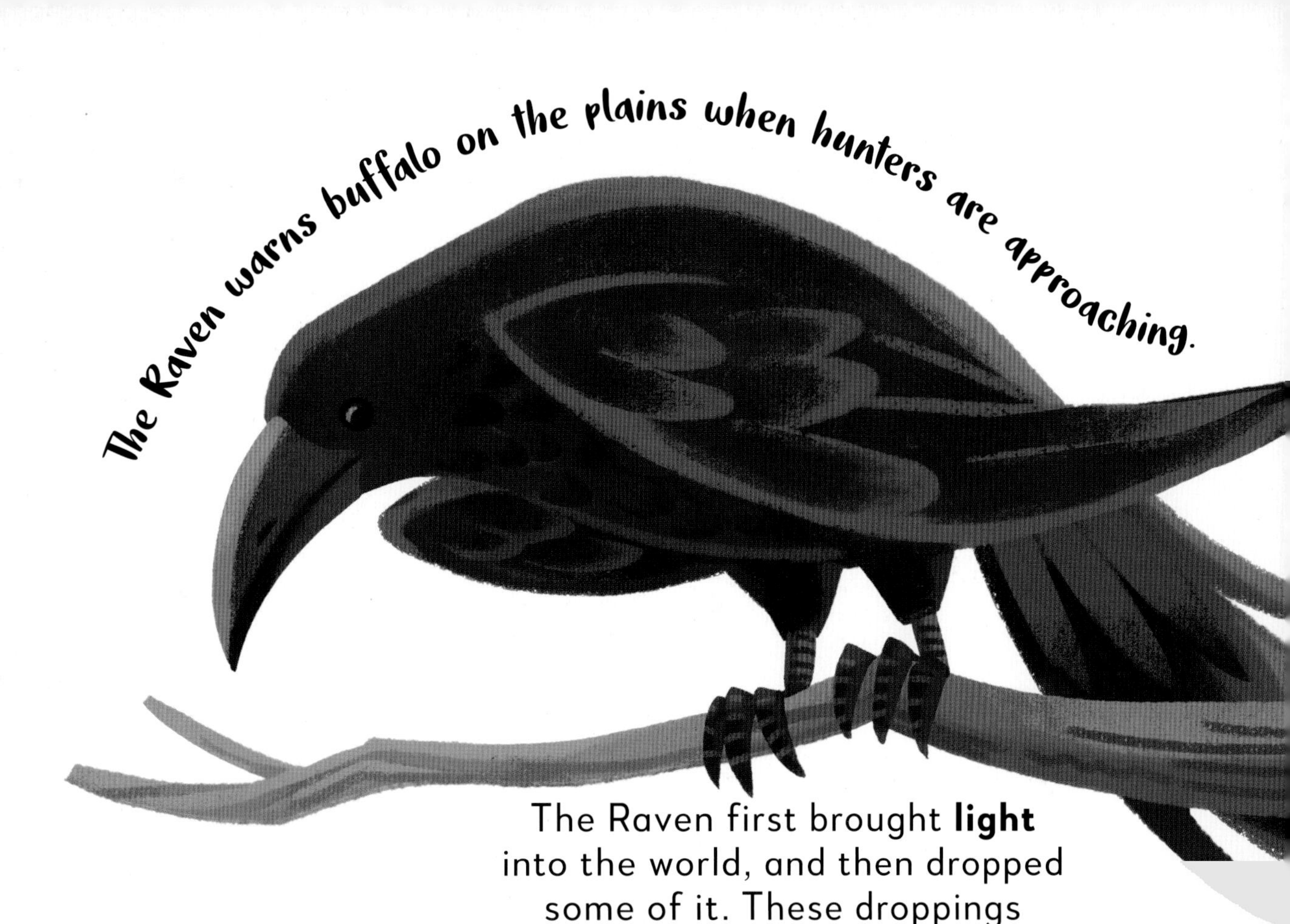

The Raven first brought **light** into the world, and then dropped some of it. These droppings became the moon and the stars.

Raven

This trickster bird of **First Nation** peoples of North America looks like an ordinary raven. But don't be fooled! It is very wise and very powerful. It can take the shape of other animals, people, or even objects.

The breadth of a roc's wings from tip to tip could be up to 80 ft (24 m).

In a story about Sinbad the sailor in *One Thousand and One Nights*, two rocs destroy Sinbad's ship by dropping huge **boulders** on it.

A roc was so big and strong it could pick up an **elephant** to eat for lunch.

Roc

Eagles are big and condors are bigger, but the roc is larger than both of them put together. Its homeland is in **Asia**, though the roc can fly anywhere it wants.

The thunderbird's place on the top of a totem pole is proof of how highly people thought of it.

If a thunderbird is angry, it can beat its wings to create a terrible storm.

The thunderbird of North American legend was known to bring **rain**—a good sign in the spring or after a drought.

Thunderbird

A thunderbird flying through the sky is hard to miss. **Lightning** flashes from its beak and **thunder** rumbles from its beating wings. With these powers it fights with spirits of the water or earth.

Fairies

Light and delicate fairies live in forests and woodland. There are **good** fairies who are helpful and kind, and there are **wicked** fairies who are always on the lookout to make trouble.

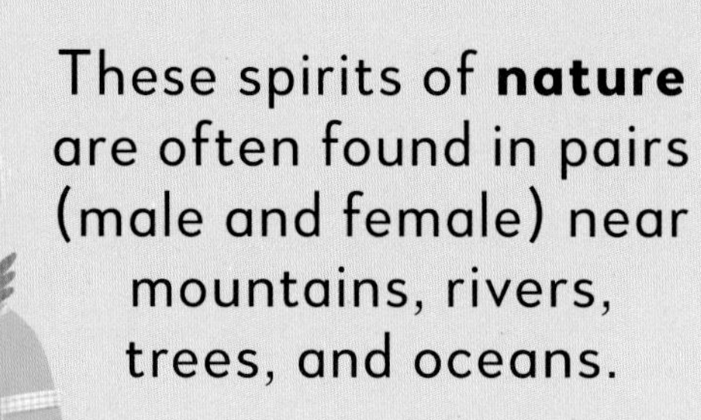

These spirits of **nature** are often found in pairs (male and female) near mountains, rivers, trees, and oceans.

Yaksha

Sprites live in forests and meadows, and are often found near **rivers** and **ponds**.

Sprite

Peri

These winged spirits from Persia like to do **good deeds**.

Fairies pop up in many **stories**, sprinkling stardust and kindness. Which of these is your favorite?

The Blue Fairy gives friendly advice to the wayward puppet, **Pinocchio**.

Blue Fairy

In the well-loved fairy story, the Fairy Godmother is **Cinderella's** kind and gentle guardian.

Fairy Godmother

Tinker Bell is **Peter Pan's** fellow traveler on his many adventures. She makes sounds like a tinkling bell.

Tinker Bell

Powerful feathered wings

In later years, Pegasus pulled the chariot of the Greek god **Zeus**.

Pegasus was tamed with the help of a golden bridle.

Pegasus

Pegasus was a horse with wings. So, he could do everything a horse could do and also fly like a bird. Pegasus was wild at first, until the Greek hero **Bellerophon** tamed him.

Moon Rabbit

Stories from China tell of the Moon Rabbit, who lives on the moon. He was brought there by the moon goddess, **Chang'e**. The Moon Rabbit once left its home to bring medicine to the sick people of Beijing.

Eshu once told the sun and the moon to swap places.

Every night, Eshu reports to the chief god **Ifa** on the news of the day.

Eshu

Eshu is a **messenger spirit** between gods in the heavens and people on earth. He knows every language there is. Eshu also likes to play tricks on people.

Eshu is best known to the **Yoruba people** who live in and around Nigeria.

Garuda

According to Hindu myth, Garuda is the **king** of all birds. He is bigger than a hawk. He is even bigger than an eagle. His beating wings are so powerful, they could stop the earth from spinning.

Powerful wings

Garuda sometimes appears as part man and part bird.

The Garuda is a **national symbol** in many countries of southern Asia.

Alicanto

Many birds eat worms, but not the alicanto of Chile. It only eats **gold** or **silver**. If an alicanto eats gold, it will give off a golden glow at night. If it eats silver, then its glow will be silvery instead.

The alicanto has difficulty flying because the gold and silver it eats make it too **heavy** to get off the ground.

The alicanto can turn off its glow if it is followed.

Itzpapalotl

Not many butterflies are fierce **warriors**. But the Aztec butterfly-goddess Itzpapalotl is different. She has bony arms and legs, and her wings are tipped with stone.

Griffin

A griffin has the head and wings of an **eagle** and the body and tail of a **lion**. Griffins are very proud of this combination. It makes them strong and powerful.

In ancient **Persia**, it was believed that griffins protected people from evil.

Griffins were known for guarding gold, and some people believed griffins laid eggs with golden **nuggets** inside.

Harpy

The harpy from ancient Greek legend has a woman's head and body, and a bird's wings and claws. Unfortunately, harpies like to **scream** and destroy things.

Harpies like to **steal** food, or sometimes even people if they get the chance!

Basan

The basan appears in stories from Japan. It looks like a large chicken—a large chicken that breathes a **cold fire**. The basan doesn't say much, but it flaps its wings a lot to make noise.

Tengu

The tengu is a **Japanese** spirit. Thousands of years ago, it looked like a dog, but later it decided to look like a bird. Nobody knows why it changed its mind.

The tengu takes its name from a doglike Chinese **demon** that first came to earth in a fiery meteor.

Tengu used to be known for fighting wars, but they later became known for doing **good deeds**.

If they're in a good mood, marids can grant **wishes**.

Marid

Jinn are magical spirits from Arabic culture, and marids are the most **powerful** of all jinn. Marids usually look like people, and they perform supernatural deeds.

Jinn of the Lamp

One famous jinn meets a boy called **Aladdin** in a story from *One Thousand and One Nights*. Aladdin rubs on the lamp to make this jinn appear. As the owner of the lamp, Aladdin becomes the jinn's master.

By rubbing on a magic ring, Aladdin meets another, lesser jinn—the **Jinn of the Ring**.

Because he is made from **fire**, Iblis thinks he is better than any human being.

Iblis

Iblis is a nasty jinn. This spirit has the power to plant an **evil** idea in the heart of a human. Does that mean people can blame Iblis for any horrible ideas they get? Some probably do.

The jann can bring **water** back to a dried-out oasis, which makes it very popular with thirsty travelers.

Janns are not as powerful as some other jinn.

Jann

A jann is an early kind of jinn that lives in the desert. It can shift its shape to fit into the desert in different ways. The jann often takes the form of either a **whirlwind** or a **white camel**.

Gagana

The Russian Gagana has feathers like other birds, but it also has an iron beak, **copper claws**, and a wingspan of almost 12 ft (4 m). Some say it is the oldest and wisest bird in the world.

Gagana guards a **magical stone** called the alatyr, which has the power to heal injuries or sickness.

Gagana lives on a mythical island called Buyan.

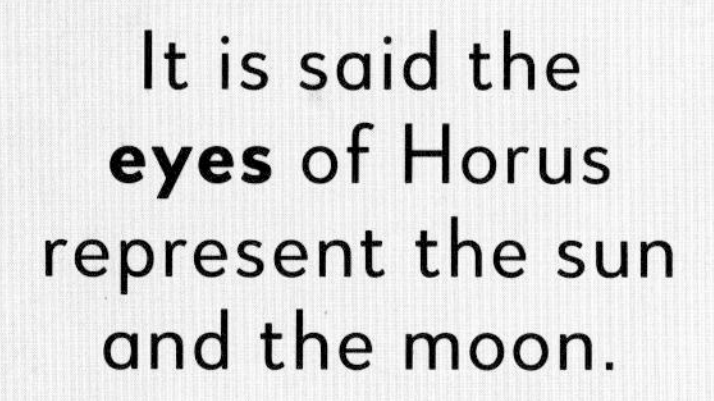

It is said the **eyes** of Horus represent the sun and the moon.

The god's great strength equals that of hundreds of humans.

Horus

Horus is the ancient Egyptian god of the sky. He is often shown with the head of a **falcon**. Horus can turn himself into many animals and can also control storms.

Chinese dragon

The magnificent Chinese dragon has a long, **snakelike** body and a big pointed head, rather like a crocodile's. This can make it look quite fierce—but it's actually very friendly!

Unlike many other dragons, most Chinese dragons don't have wings—they use their **magical powers** to fly!
Short and stubby legs
The Chinese dragon symbolizes strength and good luck.

If one of Cupid's **arrows** hits a person's heart, that person will search for love.

Cupid

Cupid is the Roman god of **love**. He looks like a child but with wings, and he tries to bring people together in love. Cupid usually means well, but sometimes he causes **mischief**.

Hippogriffs eat anything that either an eagle or a horse would eat.

Some mythical people have **ridden** on a hippogriff.

Hippogriff

The hippogriff has the front end of an **eagle** and the rear end of a horse. Its powerful wings allow it to fly very far and fast. It can even fly up to the moon.

It was Odin who gave the two ravens the ability to **talk**.

Huginn and Muninn

These two ravens from Norse myths fly all over the world and then bring news back to the chief god **Odin**. It is not their job to decide which news is worth sharing. Odin decides that for himself.

Sometimes Huginn and Muninn sit on Odin's **shoulders** while reporting back to him.

Fenghuang

Fenghuang of China is said to **rule** over all the other birds. Some say it has the head of a pheasant, the body of a duck, the beak of a parrot, and the tail of a peacock.

Simurgh

The simurgh is a giant, winged female creature from Persian myth. She has the head of a **dog**, the body of a **peacock**, and the claws of a **lion**.

The simurgh is a force for **good** in the world, and keeps both land and water pure.

The kindly simurgh serves as a link between the earth and the sky.

The **weasel** is the only animal that can stare at a cockatrice without being affected.

Cockatrice

A cockatrice looks much like a **dragon**, but with a cockerel's head and two legs. However, unlike most dragons, it cannot breathe fire.

It is widely believed that the Huma bird can never be captured.

Some stories say the Huma bird doesn't have any **legs**.

The Huma bird is said to be **invisible**, although some lucky people claim to have seen its shadow.

Jabberwock

The Jabberwock has sharp teeth, pointed claws, and flaming eyes. It also makes a lot of noise, **whiffling** and **burbling** as it moves around. This is lucky, because if you hear it, there's always plenty of time to get away.

Huma bird

The Huma bird is a sign of **good fortune**.

Many birds can fly, and some can fly high in the sky. But the Huma bird of Iranian legend is the only bird that never comes down. It spends its **whole life** soaring high above the earth.

The Jabberwock appears in a **poem** called *Jabberwocky* by English writer Lewis Carroll.

Pamola spends much of his time making sure the weather is **cold** enough to suit him.

Pamola is not happy if anyone tries to climb **Mount Katahdin** in North America.

Pamola

This Native American **thunder god** is hard to miss. He has the head of a moose, the body of a man, and an eagle's wings and claws. He protects the mountains of the **Abenaki** people.

The Peng can breathe in both air and water.

The Peng is a symbol of **strong will** and **ambition**.

Peng

The Peng is a giant Chinese bird that can change into an enormous **fish** and back again whenever it wants. It is also strong enough to fly for six months far above the ocean without resting.

Akhekh

The Akhekh became known for having a **bird's head**, an **antelope's body**, and large feathered wings. It was sometimes called the mystical serpent of evil, so it did not have many friends.

The Akhekh was at home
in **ancient Egypt**.

Akhekh was a symbol of the power of the Egyptian pharaohs.

Kukulkan

Kukulkan was a large **feathered** serpent. It was worshipped by many people, especially the Mayan people of Mesoamerica.

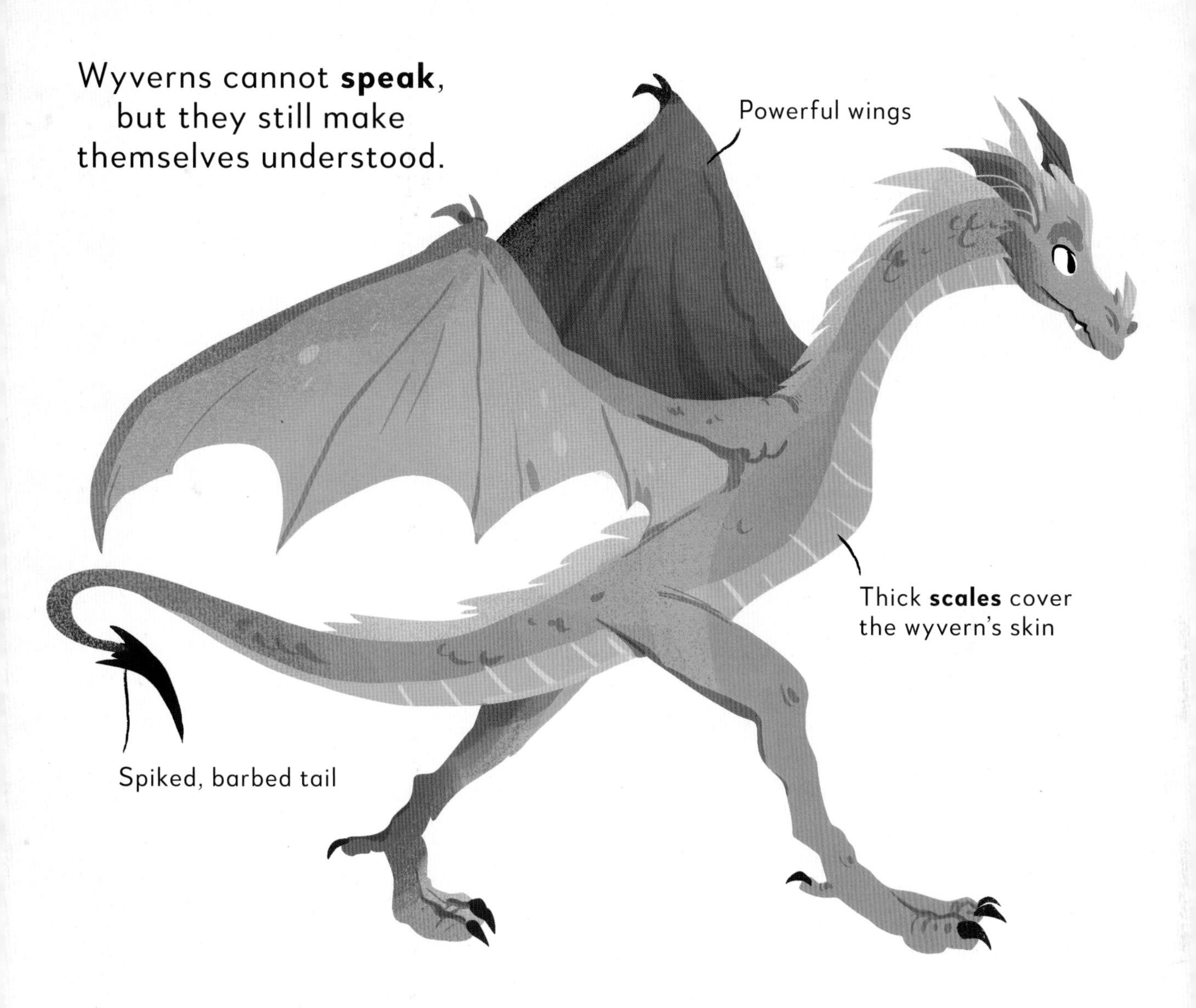

Wyvern

Most dragons have four legs. The wyvern only has two, but it also has sharp teeth, sharper claws, and a spiky, **barbed** tail.

When the king of Tonga tried to have Leutogi killed, a swarm of **bats** rescued her.

Leutogi is sometimes known as the goddess of bats. She once nursed a sick bat back to health.

Leutogi

Leutogi is a Polynesian princess known for her **kindness**. Some people thought being kind made her weak. But Leutogi continued to act as she saw fit.

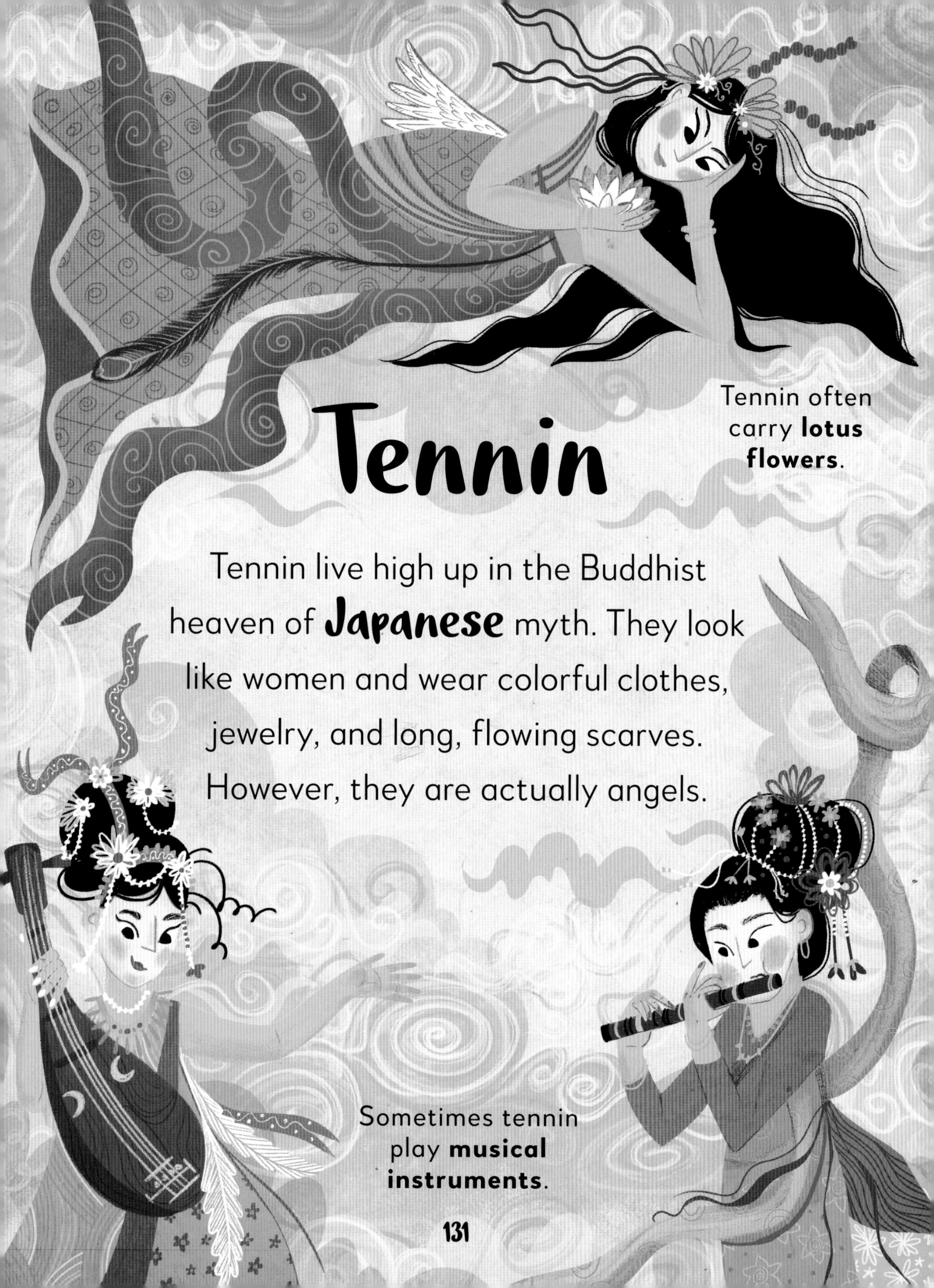

Tennin often carry **lotus flowers**.

Tennin

Tennin live high up in the Buddhist heaven of **Japanese** myth. They look like women and wear colorful clothes, jewelry, and long, flowing scarves. However, they are actually angels.

Sometimes tennin play **musical instruments**.

Tooth fairy

The tooth fairy is a very busy fairy. Every night she rushes around placing **money** under the pillows of children in return for any **baby teeth** that have fallen out.

One of the world's great **mysteries** is what the tooth fairy does with all the teeth she collects...

The Sugar Plum Fairy can take on any form she wants.

In *The Nutcracker*, a girl called **Clara** changes into the Sugar Plum Fairy.

Sugar Plum Fairy

The Sugar Plum Fairy is as **nice** as her name. She is small and **delicate**. She is also good at dancing and appears in a ballet called *The Nutcracker*.

Conclusion

The magical creatures included here might be happy or sad, curious or grumpy, and kind or mischievous. This all depends on their mood—and their mood can change without warning.

They may be big or small, have horns, spikes, pointed ears, or sharp teeth, which can all show up in the most unexpected places. True, these creatures can be placed into groups, but beyond that, they really like to go their own way.

As for what happens next, the results are never dull. And over time that's been lucky for us, because many of our stories and legends from the past are richer because these creatures have played their part.

In fact, sometimes these creatures do more than simply live in the world around us. They have been known to visit our dreams as well. For thousands of years, whether in the real or an imaginary world, they have always stood out. And if they have their way—which is what usually happens—they always will.

Glossary

Aboriginal
Relating to the Indigenous peoples of Australia

Aztecs
Native people of Mexico

charm
Magic spell or potion used on people for good or evil

conch shell
Large spiral shell

demon
Type of evil creature or spirit

devil
Evil spirit known in many religions

Dreamtime
Ancient period of time in the Australian Aboriginal religion when life was created and the world formed

evil
Wicked or very mean; the opposite of good

Gaelic
Language or culture of Ireland or Scotland

hero
brave person who takes chances for the good of other people

Hindu
Follower of Hinduism, a major religion that originated in southern Asia

immortal
Living forever

Incas
Ancient people whose empire was based in and around Peru

Jewish
Relating to the religion of Judaism and Jewish people

jinn
Also called genie, a magical spirit in Arabic culture that often grants wishes

lumberjack
Person who chops down trees and cuts them into logs

Māori
Relating to the Indigenous people of New Zealand

Mayan
Relating to the Mayan people or language of Mesoamerica

Mesoamerica
Area going south from central Mexico to Costa Rica in Central America

myth
Story or legend passed down from ancient people that often contains gods, magic, or fantastic creatures

Native American
Anything relating to the peoples who first settled in North America

Norse
Relating to the people and lands of ancient Scandinavia

Persia
Ancient empire centered in the present-day country of Iran

pharaoh
Ruler of ancient Egypt

plesiosaur
Large water-based animal that lived over 66 million years ago

serpent
Large snake

sprite
Small magical creature that lives near woods or water

symbol
Object or mark that represents a larger idea

Thousand and One Nights
Collection of stories first told in and around the Middle East

totem pole
Wooden pole decorated with carved images made by Native American people

Underworld
Mythical underground land where spirits gather after their death

Creature A-Z

Dd

Ee

Ff

Gg

Hh

Ii

Jj

Kk

Ll

Mm

Nn

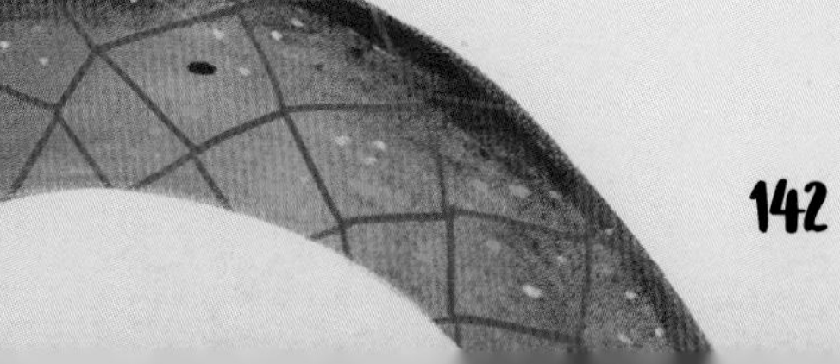

Author Stephen Krensky
Illustrators Katarzyna Doszla, Lucy Semple, Paula Zamudio, Sara Ugolotti

Senior Editor Marie Greenwood
US Senior Editor Shannon Beatty
US Editor Jill Hamilton
Designer Holly Price
Additional design Brandie Tully-Scott, Sonny Flynn
Managing Editor Jonathan Melmoth
Managing Art Editor Diane Peyton Jones
Senior Production Editor Nikoleta Parasaki
Senior Production Controller Ben Radley
Art Director Mabel Chan
Publishing Director Sarah Larter

Authenticity Consultant Bianca Hezekiah

First American Edition, 2024
Published in the United States by DK Publishing
1745 Broadway, 20th Floor, New York, NY 10019

19 20 21 22 23 10 9 8 7 6 5 4 3 2 1
001–340553–May/2024

Published in Great Britain by Dorling Kindersley Limited

A catalog record for this book is available from the Library of Congress.
ISBN 978-0-7440-9822-8

Printed and bound in China

www.dk.com

Acknowledgments

DK would like to thank: Anna Bonnerjea, Abi Maxwell, and Dawn Sirett for editorial assistance, and Caroline Hunt for proofreading.

Picture credits
1–144 123RF.com: laurent davoust for background texture